ENGLISH HANDWITING PRACTICE AND DEVELOPMENT BOOK FOR KIDS

This Book Belong To:

____

Name: Date:

In his small village, there lived a

young boy,

In his small village, there lived a

young boy,

Name: Date:

With a bright smile and eyes

full of joy.

With a bright smile and eyes

full of joy.

Name: Date:

Raj was his name, a curious

little soul,

Raj was his name, a curious

little soul,

Name: Date:

Exploring the world, he had

many stories to unfold.

Exploring the world, he had

many stories to unfold.

Name: Date:

He ran and played, with
boundless energy.

He ran and played, with
boundless energy.

Name: Date:

Discovering new things, with

childlike synergy.

Discovering new things, with

childlike synergy.

Name: Date:

Through fields and streams, he would wander,

Through fields and streams, he would wander,

Name: Date:

With a thirst for knowledge, he would ponder.

With a thirst for knowledge, he would ponder.

Name: Date:

Raj, the young boy, was a sight

to see,

Raj, the young boy, was a sight

to see,

Name: Date:

With a spirit so strong, he was

meant to be.

With a spirit so strong, he was

meant to be.

Name: Date:

A leader, a dreamer, with a

heart so kind,

A leader, a dreamer, with a

heart so kind,

Name: Date:

He was destined for greatness,

with a brilliant mind.

He was destined for greatness,

with a brilliant mind.

Name: Date:

As he grew up, his dreams

began to take shape.

As he grew up, his dreams

began to take shape.

Name: Date:

With each passing day, he

became more awake.

With each passing day, he

became more awake.

Name: Date:

A trailblazer, a visionary, with a heart of gold,

A trailblazer, a visionary, with a heart of gold,

Name: Date:

He inspired many, young and old.

He inspired many, young and old.

Name: Date:

Raj, the young boy, had become

a man,

Raj, the young boy, had become

a man,

Name: Date:

With a passion for life, and a solid plan.

With a passion for life, and a solid plan.

Name: Date:

He chased his dreams, with

courage and grace.

He chased his dreams, with

courage and grace.

Name: Date:

Leaving a mark, in this vast

human race.

Leaving a mark, in this vast

human race.

Name: Date:

With his eyes set on the horizon,

With his eyes set on the horizon,

Name: Date:

Raj embarked on a journey, with

a heart full of verve,

Raj embarked on a journey, with

a heart full of verve,

Name: Date:

He knew that he could do

anything.

He knew that he could do

anything.

Name: Date:

As long as he kept his passion

and drive alive.

As long as he kept his passion

and drive alive.

Name: Date:

He traveled far and wide,

He traveled far and wide,

Name: Date:

Through cities, towns, and

countryside,

Through cities, towns, and

countryside,

Printed by Libri Plureos GmbH in Hamburg,
Germany